THE VOYAGE
OF THE
LUDGATE HILL

TRAVELS WITH ROBERT LOUIS STEVENSON

BY NANCY WILLARD

ILLUSTRATED BY
ALICE AND MARTIN PROVENSEN

HARCOURT BRACE JOVANOVICH, PUBLISHERS
SAN DIEGO • NEW YORK • LONDON

Text copyright © 1987 by Nancy Willard
Illustrations copyright © 1987 by Alice and Martin Provensen

Requests for permission to make copies of any
part of the work should be mailed to:
Permissions, Harcourt Brace Jovanovich, Publishers,
Orlando, Florida 32887.

Library of Congress Cataloging-in-Publication Data
Willard, Nancy.
The voyage of the Ludgate Hill.
Summary: A poem inspired by Robert Louis Stevenson's
letters describes how the author and his wife survived
a stormy ocean voyage with a shipload of exotic animals.
1. Stevenson, Robert Louis, 1850–1894, in fiction,
drama, poetry, etc. 2. Children's poetry, American.
[1. Stevenson, Robert Louis, 1850–1894, in fiction,
drama, poetry, etc. 2. Sea poetry. 3. American
poetry] I. Provensen, Martin, ill. II. Provensen,
Alice, ill. III. Title.
PS3573.I444V68   1986   811'.54   86-19502
ISBN 0-15-294464–8

Printed in the United States of America
First edition   A B C D E

Quotations from Robert Louis Stevenson's letters appear courtesy
of Charles Scribner's Sons.

The paintings in this book were done in acrylic on hot press
illustration board.
The text type was set in Cochin roman with Cloister italics.
Color separations were made by Heinz Weber, Inc., Los Angeles, California.
Composed by Central Graphics, San Diego, California
Printed by Holyoke Lithograph Company, Springfield, Massachusetts
Bound by A. Horowitz & Sons, Fairfield, New Jersey
Production supervision by Warren Wallerstein
Designed by Joy Chu

HBJ

FOR THE BIRDS AND BEASTS AND ALL WHO CARE FOR THEM

—N. W.

FOR ALLELU AND JOHN KURTEN

—A. & M. P.

TO ANY READER

In August of 1887, Robert Louis Stevenson, already famous for *Treasure Island* and *The Strange Case of Dr. Jekyll and Mr. Hyde,* set sail from the port of London on a voyage to America.

Rather than sail on a "great big Birmingham liner like a new hotel," Stevenson booked passage on a cargo-carrying steamer, the *Ludgate Hill.* It was a rough crossing, but Stevenson in his letters to friends at home reveals his excitement and delight in being at sea. "O, it was lovely on our stable-ship," he wrote, obviously enjoying every minute of it.

Picture an incongruous cargo of "the baser kind of Bagman," apes and baboons, monkeys and stallions, then,

> Take all this picture, and make it roll till
> the bell shall sound unexpected notes and the
> fittings shall break loose in our state-room,
> and you have the voyage of the *Ludgate Hill.*

ONE PASSAGE ON BOARD THE STEAMSHIP LUDGATE HILL

FROM LONDON TO NEW YORK CITY, U.S.A.

Now eat your porridge, and I'll sing you the voyage

of the good ship *Ludgate Hill*.

It carried a crew of sixty and two

and a cat named Huntingtokill.

I sailed with my wife, the light of my life,
and a great many people from Dover,
but an ape in a squall made fools of us all
before the strange journey was over.

London and Scotland, good-bye!
We shall feast on mutton and pie
till light as a cork, we arrive in New York
under a buttermilk sky!

We'd hardly set sail, when my wife at the rail
heard a clatter of hooves and a bray,
and the second mate roared, "We have taken aboard
a stable and bales of hay.

No need for alarm, you shall come to no harm."
But I saw a baboon by his door
playing cards with an ape in a gabardine cape.
We were three thousand miles from shore.

Oh, buckets and brushes and bales!

Five monkeys are twitching their tails!

And confirming my fears,

I see dozens of ears

perking up at the edge of the rail.

Mrs. Early of Rood complained of the food;

her sister complained of the damp.

Mr. Collins of Greer took a chill in his ear,

and I was laid low with a cramp.

Halfway to New York we ran out of pork
and butter and biscuits and sweets,
and the cold mutton pie was in such short supply
we devoured it all in a week.

Crash and tinkle and roar!
Our dishes have flown to the floor,
and the lively baboon has run off with my spoon
and the horses are neighing for more.

We sailed for days in a lavender haze

till we met a regrettable squall.

I was tossed from my bed and knocked on the head,

and my wife had a terrible fall.

Creeping out on the deck of our wonderful wreck,
I was much astonished to see
a second baboon with a face like the moon
and a stallion as tall as a tree.

CABINS THIS WAY

Buttons and bobbins and lace!
The baboon's hearty embrace
has ruined my coat,
and I dreamed that a goat
made a meal of my traveling case.

I groped back to bed but encountered instead
a horse who admired my clothes
but decided my vest was too hard to digest
and my socks too involved with my toes.

From the hold came a rumbling, a clatter and stumbling,
the door of the stable broke free.
Mr. Collins of Greer gave chase to the mare
who was chasing five monkeys and me.

Oh, the monkeys with muttering maws!

How I long for retractable claws

and a comforting chat

with the shipmaster's cat

as she scours the pads of her paws!

When the tempest had cleared, the captain appeared

and discovered his compass and wheel

were safe with the ape in the gabardine cape

and an ancient, excitable eel.

Mrs. Early of Rood, in a generous mood,

said, "The ape has preserved us from harm.

The eel did not quail in the face of the gale.

He may go for a ride on my arm."

My wife called for fiddle and drum.

"Let them thump and twitter and thrum!

Let us skipple and hop,

and dance till we drop

or the moon changes seats with the sun!"

Mr. Collins of Greer asked if we were near,

and the captain promised us land

would dazzle our sight on this memorable night.

When a jig burst forth from the band,

the electric eel tied himself to my heel

since he could not offer his hand,

and two by two, by the light of my shoe

we skipped to the promised land.

"I was so happy on board that ship, I could not have believed it possible. We had the beastliest weather, and many discomforts; but the mere fact of its being a tramp-ship gave us many comforts; we could cut about with the men and officers, stay in the wheelhouse, discuss all manner of things, and really be a little at sea. And truly there is nothing else. I had literally forgotten what happiness was, and the full mind—full of external and physical things, not full of cares and labours and rot about a fellow's behaviour. My heart literally sang; I truly care for nothing so much as for that."

—R. L. S.

from a letter to R. A. M. Stevenson

Saranac Lake, Adirondacks

New York, U.S.A. [*October 1887*]